What happens when you

CATCH A COLD?

WHAT HAPPENS WHEN . . . ?

What Happens When You Breathe?
What Happens When You Catch a Cold?
What Happens When You Eat?
What Happens When You Grow?
What Happens When You Hurt Yourself?
What Happens When You Listen?
What Happens When You Look?
What Happens When You Run?
What Happens When You Sleep?
What Happens When You Talk?
What Happens When You Think?
What Happens When You Touch and Feel?

Library of Congress Cataloging-in-Publication Data

Richardson, Joy.
   What happens when you catch a cold?

   (What happens when— ?)
   Bibliography: p.
   Includes index.
   Summary: Describes how our bodies use their resources to fight off infections such as cold and sore throats.
   1. Cold (Disease) — Juvenile literature. [1. Immunity.   2. Cold (Disease)]   I. Maclean, Colin, 1930-   ill.   II. Maclean, Moira, ill.   III. Title.   IV. Series: Richardson, Joy.   What happens when—?
   RF361.R53   1986   616.2'05   86-3730

ISBN 1-55532-129-1
ISBN 1-55532-104-6 (lib. bdg.)
This North American edition first published in 1986 by
Gareth Stevens, Inc.
7317 West Green Tree Road   Milwaukee, Wisconsin 53223, USA

U.S. edition, this format, copyright © 1986
Supplementary text and illustrations copyright © 1986
by Gareth Stevens, Inc.
Illustrations copyright © 1984 by Colin and Moira Maclean

First published in the United Kingdom by Hamish Hamilton Children's Books with an original text copyright by Joy Richardson.

Typeset by Ries Graphics, ltd.
Series editor: MaryLee Knowlton
Cover design: Gary Moseley
Additional illustration/design: Laurie Shock

What happens when you

CATCH A COLD?

Joy Richardson

pictures by
Colin and Moira Maclean

introduction by
Gail Zander, Ph.D.

Gareth Stevens Publishing
Milwaukee

. . . a note to parents and teachers

Curiosity about the body begins shortly after birth when babies explore with their mouths. Gradually children add to their knowledge through sight, sound, and touch. They ask questions. However, as they grow, confusion or shyness may keep them from asking questions, and they may acquire little knowledge about what lies beneath their skin. More than that, they may develop bad feelings about themselves based on ignorance or misinformation.

The *What Happens When . . . ?* series helps children learn about themselves in a way that promotes healthy attitudes about their bodies and how they work. They learn that their bodies are systems of parts that work together to help them grow, stay well, and function. Each book in the series explains and illustrates how one of the systems works.

With the understanding of how their bodies work, children learn the importance of good health habits. They learn to respect the wonders of the body. With knowledge and acceptance of their bodies' parts, locations, and functions, they can develop a healthy sense of self.

This attractive series of books is an invaluable source of information for children who want to learn clear, correct, and interesting facts about how their bodies work.

GAIL ZANDER, Ph.D.
CHILD PSYCHOLOGIST
MILWAUKEE PUBLIC SCHOOLS

Oh dear!
You have caught a cold.
Where did it come from?

Colds are not caught
by getting cold.
Colds are made by germs.

If people cough or sneeze
when they have a cold,
germs shoot out into the air.

If you breathe in these germs,
you may get a cold.

7

Colds are made by
germs called viruses.
There are lots of different
viruses.
There are measles viruses
and chicken pox viruses,
flu viruses, and cold viruses.

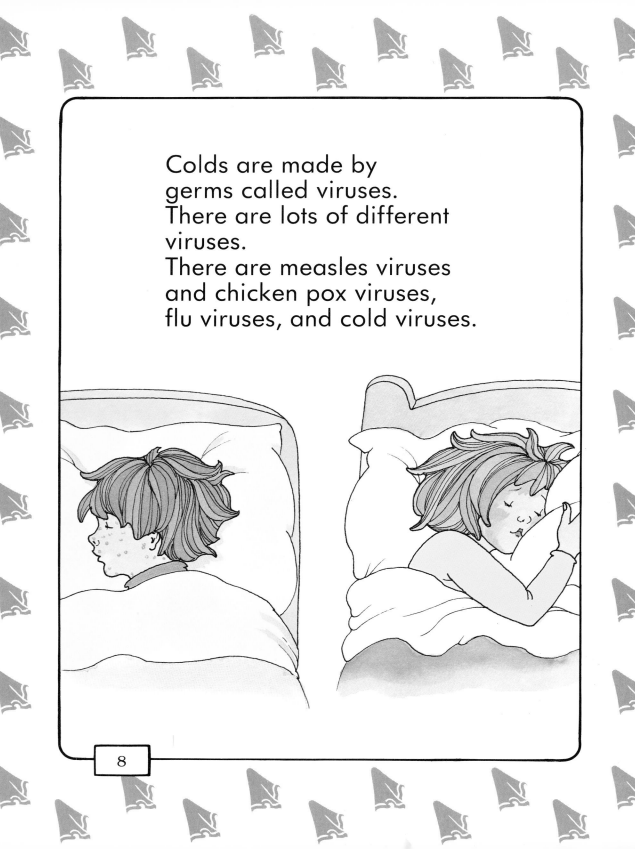

Viruses are very tiny germs.
They are too small to see with
your eyes.

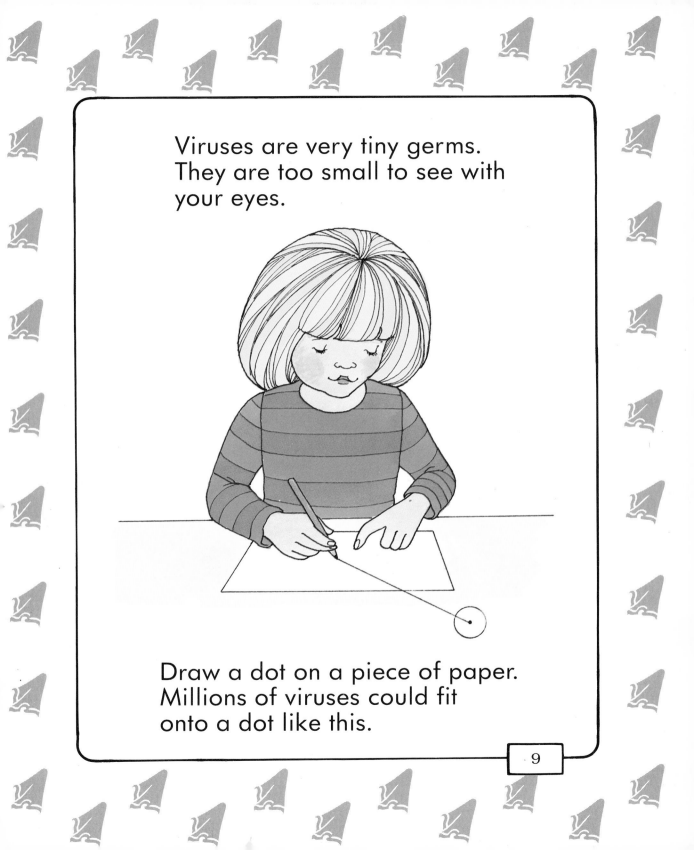

Draw a dot on a piece of paper.
Millions of viruses could fit
onto a dot like this.

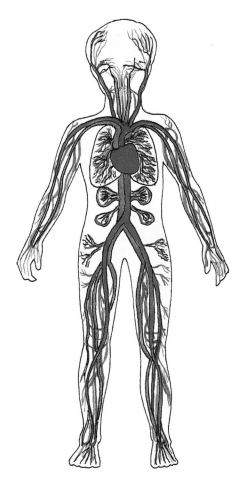

Cold viruses travel around
your body in your blood.
They look for a good place to live.
In the end, they settle down
in your nose and throat.

Your whole body is made up
of tiny parts called cells.
Cold viruses get into cells
in the walls of your nose and throat.
The viruses damage the cells.

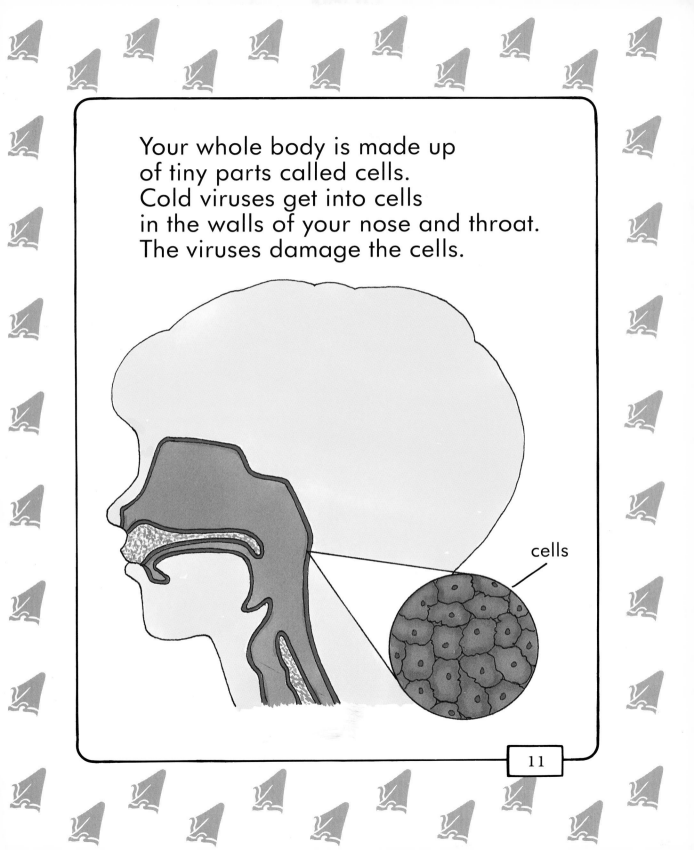

cells

Cold viruses often start work
in your throat.
They damage the cells and
make them swell up.
It hurts to swallow.

Extra blood goes to your throat.
It helps to repair the damaged cells.

Look at your mouth in a mirror.
Keep your tongue down so that
you can see the back of your throat.
Usually your throat looks dark pink.

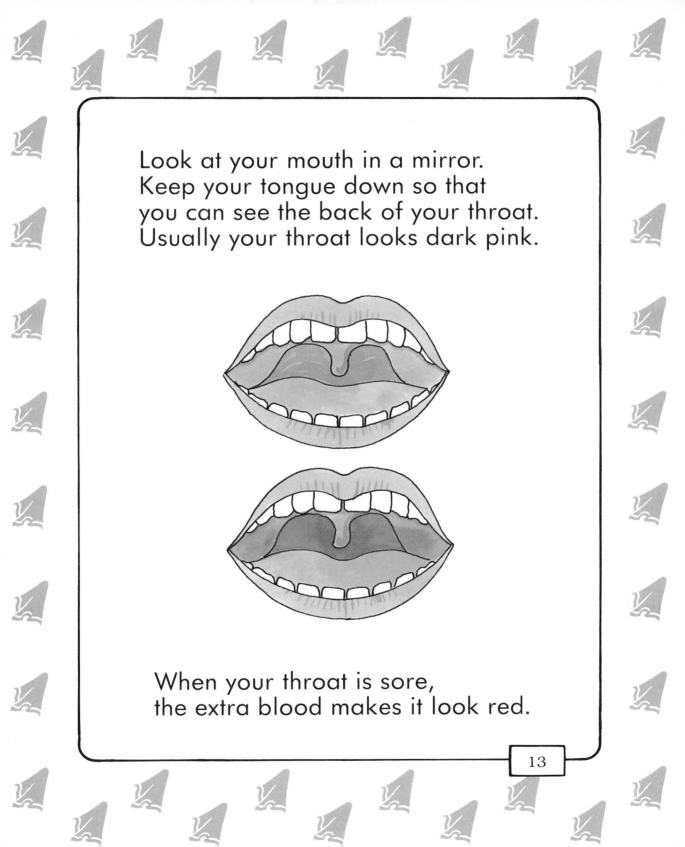

When your throat is sore,
the extra blood makes it look red.

Cold viruses make the cells in
your nose swell up, too.
Your nose feels blocked.
You have to breathe through your mouth.

Hold your nose and
read this page out loud.
Your voice sounds different
when your nose is blocked.

14

The walls of your nose make
slimy, watery stuff called mucus.
When you have a cold,
your nose makes more mucus.
Your nose runs.

Dead viruses and old cells
fall into the mucus and
make it thicker.
Your nose feels more blocked up.

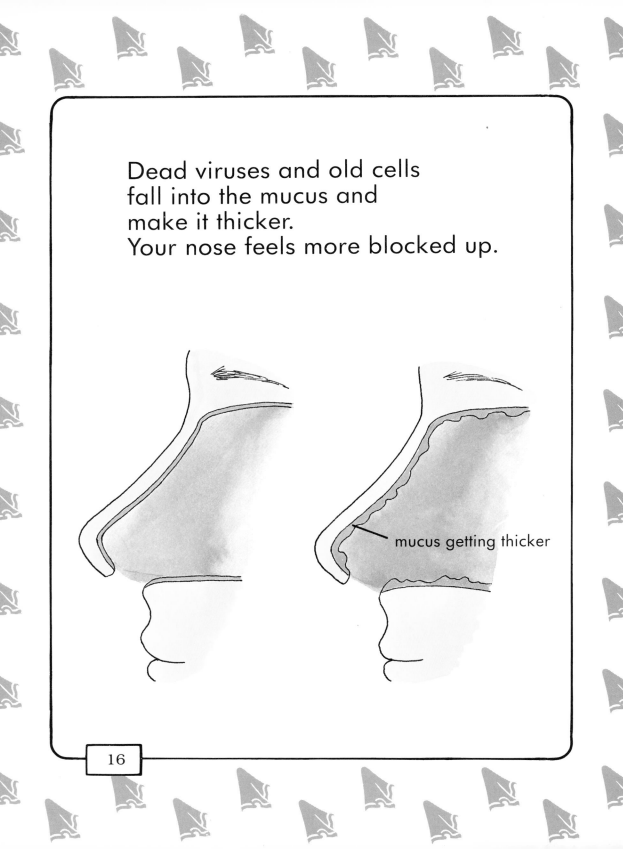

mucus getting thicker

There is a special place at the
back of your nose which you use
for smelling.
When your nose is blocked up,
you cannot smell properly.

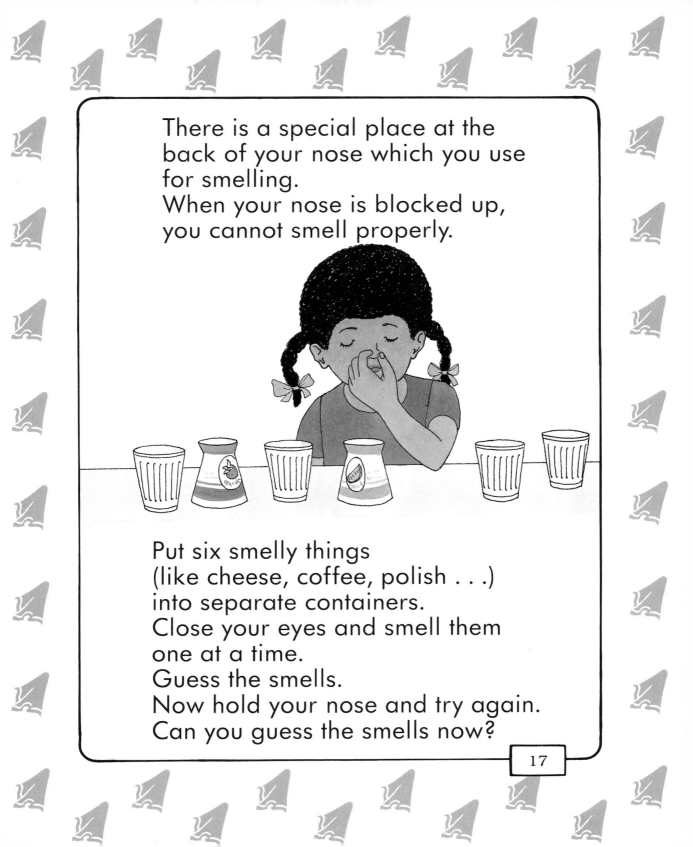

Put six smelly things
(like cheese, coffee, polish . . .)
into separate containers.
Close your eyes and smell them
one at a time.
Guess the smells.
Now hold your nose and try again.
Can you guess the smells now?

When you blow your nose,
you blow mucus out into
your handkerchief.
The rubbish gets blown out with it.

Cold viruses sometimes make
an itchy feeling inside your nose.
This makes you sneeze.
Air and mucus shoot out very fast.
The sneeze clears your nose
and stops the itch.

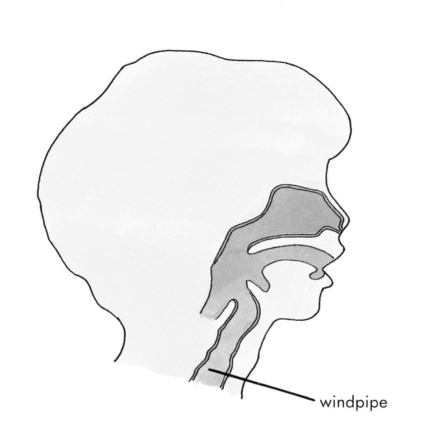

windpipe

Cold viruses often attack
the walls of your windpipe, too.
You cough to keep your windpipe clear.
Sometimes you cough
to get rid of a tickle.
Sometimes you cough up mucus.

Hold your hand over your mouth
and cough.
Can you feel the air rushing out
of your mouth?
How far away can you hold your hand
and still feel the air when you cough?

When you cough or sneeze,
germs come out in drops of mucus
along with the air.

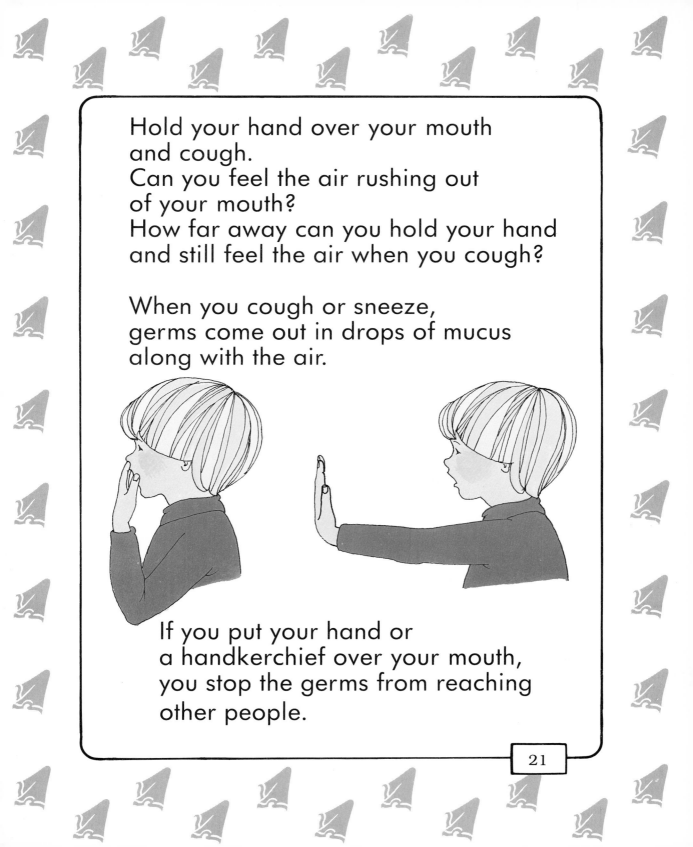

If you put your hand or
a handkerchief over your mouth,
you stop the germs from reaching
other people.

When cold viruses get into your windpipe,
they sometimes attack your voice box.
Your voice cannot work properly.
You have to talk in a whisper.

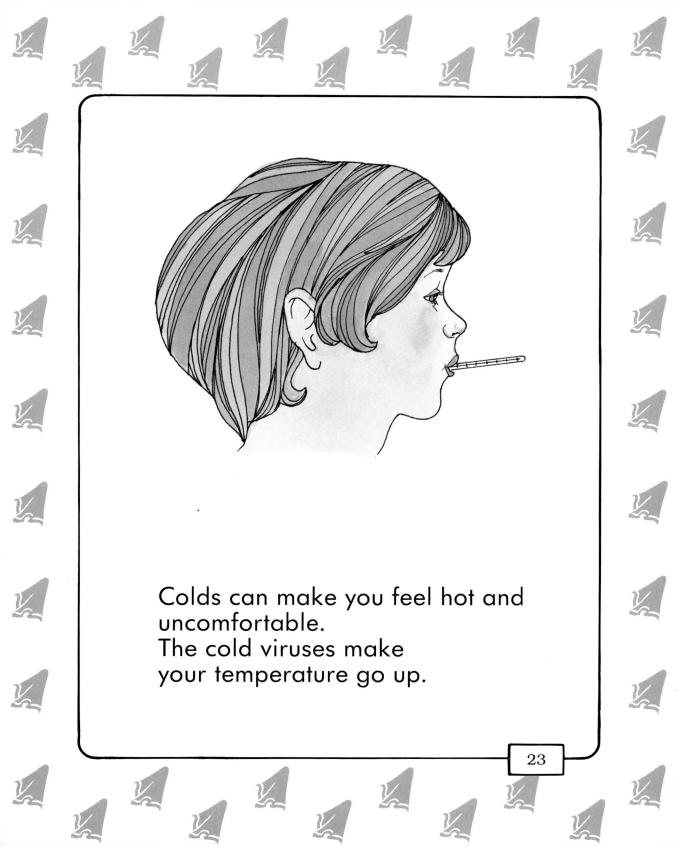

Colds can make you feel hot and
uncomfortable.
The cold viruses make
your temperature go up.

When you have a cold, medicines can help to unblock your nose or stop your coughing.

But medicines cannot get rid of the cold viruses.
Only your body can do that.

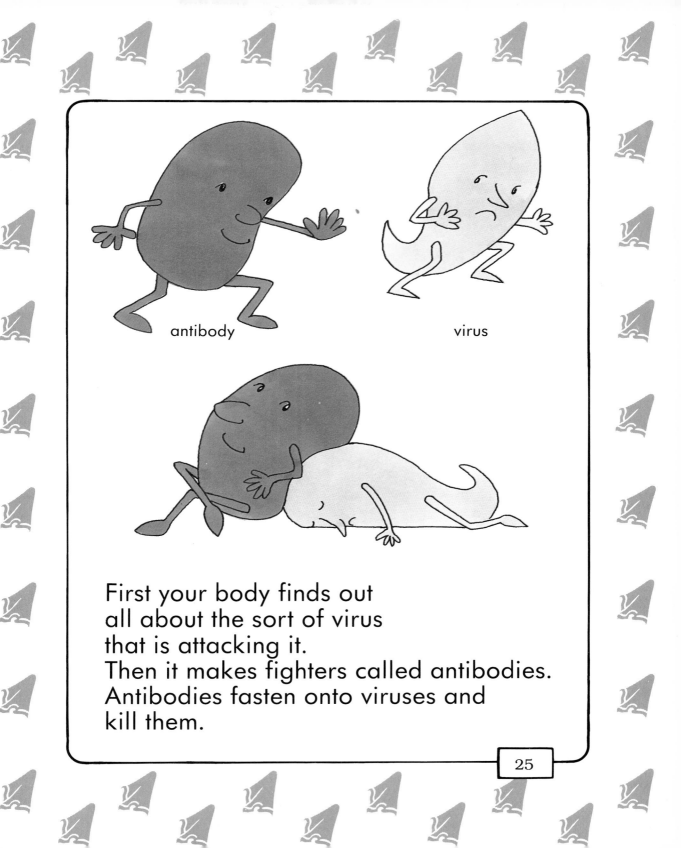

antibody

virus

First your body finds out
all about the sort of virus
that is attacking it.
Then it makes fighters called antibodies.
Antibodies fasten onto viruses and
kill them.

25

When you have had an illness,
the antibodies stay on guard.
Chicken pox antibodies stop you from
getting chicken pox again.
Measles antibodies stop you from
getting measles again.

You can get another cold because
there are different sorts of colds.
Each time you catch a new cold,
your body makes new antibodies.
They soon make you better.

People catch more colds in winter
than in summer.
In winter, the doors and windows
stay shut.
Viruses stay in the air
waiting to be breathed in.
In summer, the fresh air can blow
the viruses away.
Who can say exactly where
your cold came from?
It seems that living with people
means living with colds!

How Does That Happen?

Did you find all these things to do in *What Happens When You CATCH A COLD?* If not, turn back to the pages listed here and have some fun seeing how your body works.

1. See how small a virus is. (page 9)
2. Look at your throat in the mirror. (page 13)
3. Hold your nose and talk. (page 14)
4. Try this smelling test. (page 17)
5. Feel how germs fly when you cough. (page 21)

More Books
About Getting Sick

Listed below are more books about what happens when you get sick or catch a cold. If you are interested in them, check your library or bookstore.

Germs Make Me Sick! Berger (Crowell)

Germs Make Me Sick: A Health Handbook for Kids. Donahue/Capellaro (Knopf)

Good Health Fun Book. Aemmer (Carson-Dellos)

No Measles, No Mumps for Me. Showers (Crowell)

Patty Gets Well. Frevert (Creative Education)

Things to Know About Going to the Doctor. Marsoli (Silver Burdett)

Virus: Life's Smallest Enemies. Knight (Morrow)

Viruses. Nourse (Franklin Watts)

Where to Find More About Getting Sick

Here are some people you can write away to for more information about what happens when you get sick or catch a cold. Be sure to tell them exactly what you want to know about. Include your full name and address so they can write back to you.

Lehn and Fink Products Group
Sterling Drug, Inc.
225 Summit Avenue
Montvale, New Jersey 07645

Public Affairs Pamphlets
381 Park Avenue South
New York, New York 10016

Index

90-260

616.2
RIC

Richardson, Joy.

What happens when
you catch a cold?

$9.95

DATE DUE	BORROWER'S NAME	ROOM NO.

616.2
RIC

Richardson, Joy.

What happens when
you catch a cold?

WATERFORD GRADED SCHOOL
LIBRARY